Scholastic's The Magic School Bus®

OUT OF THIS WORLD

A Book About Space Rocks

SCHOLASTIC INC.
New York Toronto London Auckland Sydney

Based on the episode from the animated TV series
produced by Scholastic Productions, Inc.
Based on *The Magic School Bus* book series
written by Joanna Cole and illustrated by Bruce Degen

TV tie-in adaptation by Jackie Posner and illustrated by Robbin Cuddy.
TV script written by Libby Hinson and George Arthur Bloom.

ISBN 0-590-92156-8

12 11 10 9 8 7   7 8 9/9 0 1/0

Printed in the U.S.A.   23

First Scholastic printing, October 1996

Having a teacher like Ms. Frizzle can be out of this world! Take yesterday, for example, when we were rehearsing for our solar system play. Suddenly a loud crash came from the hallway. We raced to the door to find Ms. Frizzle and Dorothy Ann on the floor.

Rushing to class, Dorothy Ann had run smack into the Friz. Books, films, and papers were everywhere!

"Well, as I always say, there's nothing like starting the day with a bang!" exclaimed Ms. Frizzle as she and Dorothy Ann dusted themselves off.

"Where have you been, Dorothy Ann?" asked Wanda. "We had to start our solar system play without you."

"Yeah, you're supposed to be Pluto," Carlos said. "Arf, arf!" he joked.

"There's no time for a play!" cried Dorothy Ann. "We have to evacuate the school this instant! I've been tracking an asteroid I saw through my telescope."

"What's an asteroid?" Tim asked.

"It's a big space rock," Dorothy Ann answered. "And according to my calculations, sometime in the next twenty-four hours it's going to crash into our school and destroy it!"

"How are we going to find out if D.A. is right?" asked Phoebe worriedly. We all had the same thought.

That's when Ms. Frizzle got a sparkle in her eyes. "As my old astronomy teacher used to say: Star light, star bright — there's always a way to find out if you're right! To the bus, class!"

Oh no! A field trip to outer space!

"Welcome, crew of the Magic Space Bus," announced Ms. Frizzle as our old school bus changed into a Space Bus. "Our mission today is to find Dorothy Ann's mysterious space object, follow its path, and if necessary keep it from crashing into Walker Elementary!"

And off we went!

We had just taken off when suddenly something zoomed by. We raced to the window, but it had already burned out.

"Maybe that was Dorothy Ann's asteroid," said Keesha hopefully.

"No, it was a shooting star!" Phoebe said.

"That's right. But shooting stars are meteors — space rocks," explained Ms. Frizzle. "Most meteors burn up when they enter Earth's atmosphere."

"And," added Dorothy Ann, "according to my observations, my asteroid is much bigger and is coming from the direction of Saturn."

Ms. Frizzle shouted some commands at Liz, our pilot. Before we knew it, we were zooming off toward Saturn.

Suddenly we noticed we were off course. We all fell to the right.

"What's happening?!" we yelled.

"We're about to cross paths with the Moon!" exclaimed Dorothy Ann.

We all rushed to the window. Sure enough, the Space Bus was heading right toward the Moon! We were going to crash!

"But we were heading toward Saturn — not the Moon!" pointed out Keesha. "What changed our path?"

Just when we thought we were moondust, Dorothy Ann looked up from her map. "I figured it out," she announced. "Because the Moon is so much bigger than we are — we're being pulled in by its gravity!"

"Can't we just change our path?" asked Phoebe.

"Right on track, Phoebe," responded the Friz. "I suggest an orbital insertion burn."

"In other words, step on it!" Carlos said.

Liz pressed some buttons. In no time at all the Space Bus was traveling on a path around the Moon instead of into it!

It was getting late. We had to find Dorothy Ann's asteroid before it hit our school! That's when we realized we were stuck in a path around the Moon.

"Is it just me, or are we playing ring around the Moon?" asked Ralphie.

Just then a small space rock zipped by. It was heading straight for the moon! Kaboom! The space rock smashed into the Moon and exploded.

When a space rock *does* crash into something, it's called a meteorite.

The Moon has taken a creaming but keeps on beaming!

"That meteorite proves my point," cried Dorothy Ann, her nose in her map. "Things still crash into each other, even though there's a lot of room out here in space!"

"And if that meteorite had crashed into our school instead of the Moon," explained Ms. Frizzle, "it would've been good-bye Walker Elementary."

Finally, Liz pulled the Space Bus out of its path around the Moon. Then Wanda saw something fly by her window. "I think I see your asteroid!" she exclaimed.

Dorothy Ann rushed over to Wanda. "Wait a second," she said. "It's got a tail, which means it's a comet! I don't think what I saw through my telescope was a comet."

Comets, meteorites, asteroids... where do they come from?

They're just bits of space junk that were left over after the planets formed.

That comet looks more like a scoop of rocky road ice cream than a rock!

Dorothy Ann wrinkled her nose. "Gee, maybe this comet is what I saw!" she sighed as she looked out the window. "Now I'm not sure."

"I say we blast it to smithereens!" exclaimed Carlos.

Phoebe remembered that a comet is made of ice and rock. "We don't have to blast it," she explained to Carlos. "We can melt it."

Dorothy Ann wanted us to wait to melt the comet, but we were losing time. Soon it would be out of range.

"Extend the megareflector, Liz!" ordered Wanda. "And begin meltdown!" The sun reflected off a giant mirror, and suddenly the comet began to melt.

"We got it!" we cheered.

"All the rock and dust are coming off and evaporating," noted Keesha.

"And the dust is making the tail bigger and brighter," continued Tim.

How does it feel to have saved Walker Elementary from destruction?

No comet.

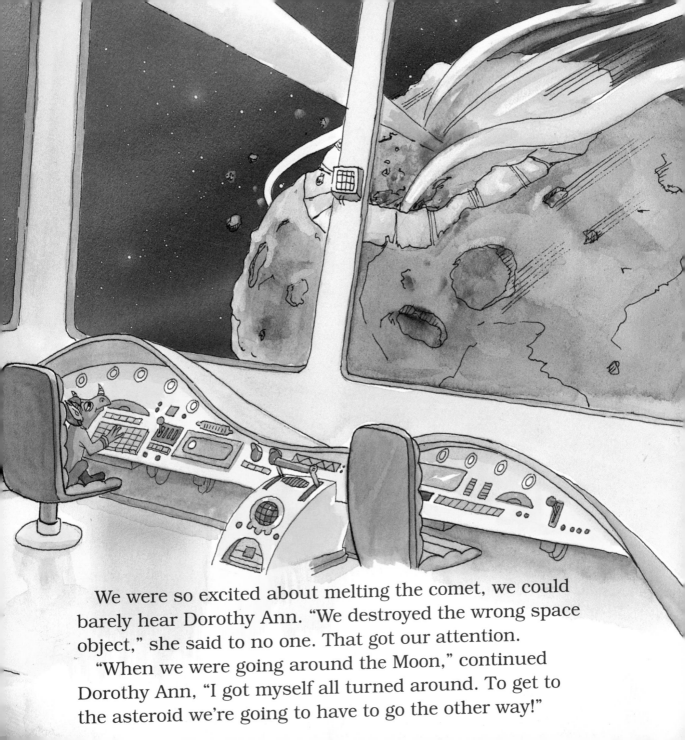

We were so excited about melting the comet, we could barely hear Dorothy Ann. "We destroyed the wrong space object," she said to no one. That got our attention.

"When we were going around the Moon," continued Dorothy Ann, "I got myself all turned around. To get to the asteroid we're going to have to go the other way!"

Liz quickly turned the Space Bus around. Before we even settled into our seats, Dorothy Ann spotted a huge space rock outside our window. "There it is!" she announced.

"WHOAAA! That's one big space rock!" cried Tim.

Finally face to face with the asteroid, we had grown a little nervous. How were we ever going to get rid of it? we wondered.

Is it just me, or is the asteroid not melting?

"If we could melt a comet, how hard could it be to melt an asteroid?" reasoned Arnold.

We tried and tried to melt the asteroid, but it just wouldn't melt!

"It looks like it's made of metal," noticed Tim.

"Metal and rock, to be exact," responded Ms. Frizzle.

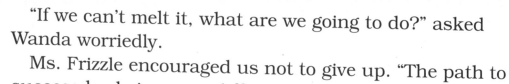

"If we can't melt it, what are we going to do?" asked Wanda worriedly.

Ms. Frizzle encouraged us not to give up. "The path to success leads in many different directions."

"That's it!" exclaimed Dorothy Ann. "We don't need to destroy the asteroid. We just need to change its path so it doesn't hit our school!"

WAAAAAAAHOOOOOOO!!!

Then Carlos came up with a great idea. He had noticed earlier that the Space Bus had a two-seater space pod that could detach from the Space Bus. And now was the perfect time to use it!

He told us that attached to the space pod was a rammer-slammer magnet. With the magnet, the space pod could be attached to the metallic asteroid. Once attached, the space pod's rockets could pull the asteroid off course.

With the Friz as co-captain, Carlos pulled on his space helmet.

"Ready to launch!" announced Wanda, hand on the launch lever.

"LAUNCH!" exclaimed Dorothy Ann. And off they went.

"Arm the rammer-slammer magnet!" shouted Ms. Frizzle as the asteroid came into view.

"Here we go!" Carlos called out.

From inside the Space Bus, we watched the space pod attach itself to the asteroid.

Oh bad oh bad oh bad bad bad!

Then Carlos and Ms. Frizzle fired the space pod's rockets. They tried and tried to move the asteroid. But it wouldn't move!

"The space pod's rockets aren't powerful enough to pull the asteroid out of its path!" exclaimed Dorothy Ann in a panic.

Then we noticed that the Friz and Carlos couldn't pull the magnet off the asteroid. It was stuck! What were we going to do?

Just when we thought we were doomed, Phoebe jumped up from her seat. "If the Space Bus becomes bigger and heavier than the asteroid, wouldn't our gravity pull it into a path around us?" she asked.

"Terrific! Then we can baby-sit the asteroid for the rest of our lives!" responded Wanda.

"Not if we get rid of it!" cried Dorothy Ann. She knew exactly what to do.

Get rid of the asteroid?

Here's how we can do it.

Dorothy Ann drew a picture of a huge Space Bus with the asteroid traveling in a path around it. "If we get very big the asteroid will swing around us," she explained as she pointed to her diagram.

On another piece of paper she drew a tiny Space Bus. "If we get small again, we'll lose our gravitational pull. Then we'll send the asteroid flying into the Sun and it'll be gone forever!" She sketched the asteroid flying off the page.

I have a plan.

We thought Dorothy Ann's idea sounded out of this world. Except, what about Carlos and Ms. Frizzle?

Leave it to Dorothy Ann to work this out, too. "Maybe they can't get the pod off the asteroid, but they can escape the pod," she said.

With the plan all mapped out, Dorothy Ann got on the microphone to explain it to Ms. Frizzle.

The asteroid moved closer and closer to Earth — and to our school. We had to work fast.

"You have to make this bus as big and heavy as you can!" Dorothy Ann instructed Liz.

"At least as heavy as the Moon!" Arnold added.

The Space Bus shook and heaved. Before we knew it, we went from the size of a comet to the size of an asteroid, until finally we were as big as the Moon.

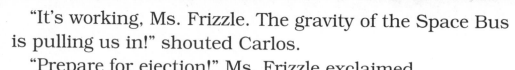

"It's working, Ms. Frizzle. The gravity of the Space Bus is pulling us in!" shouted Carlos.

"Prepare for ejection!" Ms. Frizzle exclaimed.

Meanwhile, inside the Space Bus, we opened the hatch to let them in.

"Eject!" yelled the Friz.

And in they flew.

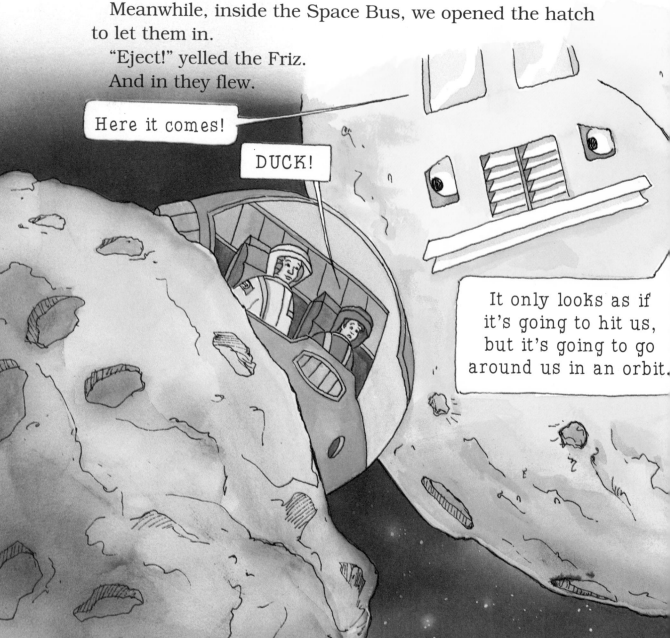

Now, all we had to do was get smaller at just the right time and send that asteroid on a path into the Sun.

Dorothy Ann explained everything to Liz. "Shrink us back to normal size and release the asteroid from our gravitational pull."

"You can do it, Liz," encouraged Wanda. "You've got the right stuff!"

"Ten seconds to release," announced Dorothy Ann.

We gathered around Liz and counted together. "Ten . . . nine . . . eight . . . seven . . . six . . . five . . . four . . . three . . . two . . . one! Release!" Kapow!

"We did it!" we cheered as we shrank back to normal size. We watched the asteroid zoom toward the Sun.

"Way to go, Lieutenant Liz!" exclaimed Dorothy Ann, patting her on the head.

Mission accomplished, Ms. Frizzle directed the Space Bus toward Earth. "Prepare for reentry!" she exclaimed. "We're going home!"

Briiing! Briing!

Magic School Bus: Hit the speakerphone, Liz. Hello, Magic School Bus.

NASA: This is NASA calling. I understand you were trying to reach us.

Magic School Bus: Well, actually the kids were trying to reach you.

NASA: Understood. Well, we just read your book about space rocks. And we liked it.

Magic School Bus: Really?

NASA: However, for the future, not all asteroids are magnetic.

Magic School Bus: Well, we, uh . . . we know that. But some are made of iron and nickel and those *are* magnetic. Right?

NASA: Yes. And some are made of stone — and those *aren't* magnetic, so let's just make that clear! All right?

Magic School Bus: Gulp! Yes, madame.

NASA: Another thing! It would've taken weeks for the asteroid to reach the Sun. You made it seem like it could happen in seconds!

Magic School Bus: We, uh . . . we had to fake it. Our book is only about 30 pages long. What could we do?

NASA: Well, okay. And one last thing. If your kids were *really* in a Space Bus, they'd be floating around, not walking around. But we probably know the reason why you did that—you had to fake it, right?

Magic School Bus: Right! (Phew!)

From the desk of Ms. Frizzle

Meteors and comets are bits and pieces of rock left over after the planets formed. When a space rock crashes into something, it's called a meteorite. Although meteorites have hit our planet in the past, it only happens once in a very great while. The chances of one even landing on your school are maybe once in a million years.

Large meteorites that have hit Earth have caused serious problems. Some scientists even believe that a very large meteorite may have caused the extinction of dinosaurs!

Comets are different from meteorites. They are made up of ice as well as rock. They have tails, and they melt whenever their orbits take them too close to the Sun. But if you wanted to melt one from here on Earth, you'd need a pretty gigantic mirror

Ms. Frizzle